Unique-ly Written

"WE MUST PLANT OUR SEED IN LIFE, NUTURE IT,

ONCE ITS GROWTH IS ABUNDANT,

THE TRUE BEAUTY IS REVEALED!"
                                    -T.COOPER

Tiffany Cooper

authorHOUSE®

AuthorHouse™
1663 Liberty Drive
Bloomington, IN 47403
www.authorhouse.com
Phone: 1-800-839-8640

First published by AuthorHouse   2/15/2011

ISBN: 978-1-4567-1961-6 (sc)
ISBN: 978-1-4567-1960-9 (hc)
ISBN: 978-1-4567-1959-3 (e)

Library of Congress Control Number: 2010919293

Printed in the United States of America

Dedication

This book is dedicated to my children: John, Tomier, and Cy'Ani Cooper. My sister, Latrice Howard, my niece and nephew: TaCoya and Khalif Dalton, and my Mother, Linda Greene. Thank you all for your support throughout life's many struggles and successes! I love you all!

Acknowledgments

First, I give all glory and thanks to God and Lord Jesus Christ our Savior for without them in my life I am nothing. I am a work in progress; all that is being done is truly a blessing. My children John (JB), Tomier (Tommy), Cy'Ani (Cy-Cy) it is because of the three of you I strive for more. You are the core of my joy. Mother (Linda), you have been an example of a strong, independent woman, you have been a mother, father, and friend. You always told me to know my worth: I am a "STAR". Thank you for teaching me what it means to be a woman of substance, I love you! My sister (Latrice), my best friend, my rock, I love you beyond measures. I respect and honor the daughter, mother, sister, and woman that you are. Thank you for giving me your unconditional love & being by my side thru and thru! My brother (Billy), I love you. TaCoya & Khalif, Aunt Tiff loves you more than you know thank you for helping and sharing special times with me, putting many smiles upon my face . Nyair (Ny-Boogie/handsome), Auntie Tiff loves you "Go Ny, Go Ny!" (lol). Kendaya (Daya), it's been too long; know that you hold a place in my heart I Love you always and forever.

Theresa (Aunt Princess), you call me "Sunshine", I am glad that you are a part of my life's rainbow, much love Boss Lady. Aunt Edie and Aunt Jackie love you ladies thank you for your love and support. Lasonia, thank you for hanging in there with me, love you. Bettina (Mom Tina), thank you for the many talks, you have taught me a lot which never went unnoticed I have so much love and admiration for you. Dorian ("D"), my friend of 31 years you mean so much to me thank you for being you, staying true to me always, love you forever man! Mr. Manns (Gus), my friend of 30 years, thank you for your realness. Your friendship holds much weight "You a Mess"(lol) you know how we get down love you always. Ms. Davis (Vickie), you are one of not many that

I consider my truest friends I love you for never changing, always keeping it real and keeping the hair fly!(lol) the respect I have for you has no limit, thank you. Lisa, whenever I call---you answer, I appreciate you. Thank you for loving me no matter what. To all my family too many to name who always supports me in everything I set out to do thank you & I Love You. To all I may have not mentioned however I've already verbally acknowledged your love and support and the love I hold for you thank you. I appreciate everybody who genuinely believes in me even at times when I didn't believe in myself nor my talents. To ALL who have JUDGED me or who are still JUDGING me THANK YOU. It's been a long time coming yes my change is here, getting it done one day at a time!

Contents

Savor Being Erogenous 89

Unravel Perceptions

"We should ACKNOWLEDGE our FEELINGS; bask in the defining EXPERIENCES. There are a variety of ways to express the VALUE and gratification one may get out of each scenario."

-Unique

PRICELESS IMAGES

Icicles, white snow
From the rooftops
Observing the scenery below
Trees covered, dams flowing
Winter storming, nightlights gleaming
Ponds smoothly iced
Streets at a stand still
Images remembered
Priceless images of winter!

THE CANVAS

A canvas of love's multi-colors
The pattern, a masterpiece rich in realness
Details meaningful-
Sketched to the imagination of the beholder
Distinctively blended the sway of each color
With only a commendable glimpse
It unleashes the canvas of love's symphony
In which the art adorns the heart!

First Kiss

Golden skinned tone
Head to toe
Mixed up in your tide
About to explode
The warm touch
Of your hands on my side
Blows my mind
Steady in pace
All up in my face
Your tender lips
Touching mines
Gaped into my eyes
Enjoying the significance
That's what was wanted
Nothing too complex
Only an innocent and gentle kiss!

Love's Breeze

Love mounted another day
The beauty is within
Halt, feel it,
It's in the spew of the wind
Inhale, be liberated
That's when you'll know
Love has taken over
Taken over your being!

Hold Her

Hold her
Cling tight
Give her the security
Everything is alright
Before closing her eyes
It'll be you
She'll kiss good-night
Hold her
Until morning
Awakened by the sun together
Those moments she'll cherish forever!

Proud

The smile upon your face
Uttering you're proud
Witnessing where I was where I am today
A safe haven filled with possibilities
No hassles No worries
Your friend forever that lady
In need to talk or vent
Sincerely, I've given my commitment
A special friend to this
Don't ever forget it
Potential there from the start
UNIQUE, the one with the big heart
Proud!

What is Love?

What is love?
Feelings appeasing
Is it pain, peace, misery?
Is it delight with you or me?
This thing we call love
Is it meant to be?
Sentiments of what you undergo
Detoured at times for love
Once again,
Longing that thing we call love
Love & its complexity can be boggling
Searching what it is
You're mind is being challenged!

My Friend

Friendship with you
I'm extricated to be me
You're my escape my real life fantasy
You're the person I'm comfortable around
Who'd knew,
We'd always hold each other down
The simple things we do
Conversation is great
Time bestowed never compared
Here's to you!
Thank you for being a friend
Thank you for always being there!

Sister

Latrice, my one and only sister
We have a bond
That's right
Disagreements, dislikes
We never fight
Tears and smiles
I look up to you
I appreciate you
When you have no words no opinion
I respect and admire you
I'm driven
I'm in a different place
An enormous bulk of love
In my heart forever is just your space
Latrice, my one and only sister
I honor you
For being loving to me
And being you
Forever my sister
Always staying true!

Moment's Time

For only a moment's time
You lay resting
Where you're at, who you're with
She's your escape
With no care in the world
For only a moment's time
She's you're girl
The scent of your cologne
In the air she breathes
Although you're not always there
Your essence remains
For only a moment's time
You're there as you should be
With her
No drama No confusion
A moment's time of intimacy!

Love Kept

Love, center of all
Kindness, loyalty, sorrow, joy
Words building a wall
Oh boy, if it's in your soul
Open up let someone in
Feelings intense
Love, center of all
Holding back watching your step
There's no option
You're detained
Love keeper, Love kept
Love has no place to go
It's contained it can't hide
Love never left behind!

Beautiful Love

I once wrote a poem about a love
Beautiful as a white dove
Some wondered was it
What you call pure everlasting love
Described so simply yet complex
More to it than sex
Communication the key
Trying to define the intensity
When looking love in the front
Seeking understanding to this love
That was brought into my life
Rare a love extraordinary
Has taken me emotionally
Somewhere I'd never been before
An experience of a lifetime
I didn't want to end
I wanted this beautiful love
Curious to what was in store!

My Sister and My Mother

Embracing strength & courage
From My sister & My mother
For them, my love is infinite
They are my true friends
Holding no punches No need to pretend
Wanting the best for me
The ultimate endowment the ultimate gratification
My sister & My mother
Nobody replaces them
They pick me up if and when I'd fall
With their love and guidance surrounding me
I aim to better Tiffany
The level in the building called "Respect" stands tall
My sister & My mother
The two women who mean everything to me
My all!

Vow

Vowing to be in each of our lives
Today, tomorrow, forever
Husband and wife
One love meant to be
An incredible destiny
Honoring the commitments and vows
Thru all ups and downs
Trusting in each other and the Lord
No woman, man, or thing
Will take us under
'til death do us part
Welcoming this union with great value
Into our heart!

Gesture of Love

Dedicating this poem to my cousin
Courtney Greene
A small gesture of my love
Letting you know what you truly mean
Watching you grow from a baby to a boy
Boy to a teen
I moved away missing your teenage years
In my heart you remained always near
I'm amazingly proud of the young man you've become
We know there's a special angel named
"Daddy- Bubby"
That watches over you from above
He'd be overjoyed you're his son
Courtney Greene You Are Loved!
Hold on to knowing you are ever so Blessed
You keep on passing God's given test
You've worked hard t get to where you are today
You don't owe anybody anything
Except God who has given you the gift in a special way
I want to see you soar
Exceed your own expectations
I'll watch your games as I've always before from afar
Do me a favor
Never forget
Where you came from, where you've been, who you are
You did it!!

Although your journey may not have been easy
You finish college
Now you're in the NFL
How pleasing
Congratulations!

Support

He's focused not on you
Due to there's things he has to do
Don't be selfish
Just be the one who'll see him thru
If he truly cares
He will be there
Stop listening to your girls
Live your own world
Learn from your own mistakes
Being in love is a chance
We all take
Don't be afraid
Your heart does what your mind tells it to
Know that whatever the results
Was never up to him or you!

Trying Times

"Everybody has them at some point or another; these times are what BUILDS our CHARACTER, allowing one to gain WISDOM."

-Unique

Choices

To lead not follow
Not ruin yet create
Be insightful not ignorant
Never stagnate always fluent
Don't lie be truthful
Choices we make
Know when to stand up not sit down
Wear a smile not a frown
Know when to speak or be silent
Calm not rowdy
Don't give up always keep trying
Weigh the options
The pro's and the con's
There's a cause and effect to every decision
To give to take
Listen or ignore
Be loyal not cheat
Smoke, eat, or drink
To love not hate
Everyday choices we must make!

Be Careful

Trying to exemplify what's within
Maybe he'd be the one
He'll bring with him the sun
You jump up, there was no one
How could it be, he was an illusion in your dreams
Time to go in with your lens
Focused on the prize
Start a new chapter in your book called "Life"
Take no static
Don't give your heart too quick
Be sure this time it's legit
Better to be friends 1st than lovers
You already know a love thing
Can be a struggle
Handle with care
Is it your lover or your friend!

Jealousy

Jealousy, envy not known in my vocabulary
Happiness, success
I've experienced to be best
It's never too late
To make a fresh start
Nobody's perfect
Try to change indifferent ways
Deserving better days
Keep an open mind to it all
How much joy it brings
Jealousy, envy will set you up to fall!

Angry Eyes

The anger in your eyes is unexplainable
The anger in your eyes, what's bothering you?
What can your Mother do?
You have it captive, what has come over you?
To self be true-
Take responsibility for the right AND wrong that you do
'Cause this anger in your eyes,
It's not you.
Baffled for words
Your anger is your hurt
Let the pain be subdued, progress forward, no doubts.
Life has its ups and downs
What goes around comes around
To love is to live.
To live is to love.
Put your hands together, kneel down
Pray to the man above!

Confused

Sometimes when you're down and out
Needing to be alone
Nobody understands the sentiment shown
It's difficult to interpret
Confused
Not knowing what to do
With the thoughts on your mind
Happiness you can't find
What makes it go wrong?
Life has been a sad love song
Unwanted is what you feel
Wanting success in all things
To be something, somebody, one day to feel again
Having dreams you want to follow
If only the fear you could swallow
Confused,
However, far from being a person who is shallow!

Misunderstood

Misunderstood in your appearance
Do they look beyond the appeal of your flesh?
Taking you as you are
With no assumptions
The past gone far
Love bares all
That's what has been said
Misunderstood in your appearance
Awaiting an companion your friend
Without love
What is it really about in the end
Wanting love beyond the surface
Loving someone other than self
What good is love if you're by yourself?

Liar Liar

Liar Liar why?
Why do you lie the way you do
It's a damn shame how you lie
What's wrong with you
You should be in the Hall of Fame
You know who you are
No need to say your name
Liar liar, what's the problem
You lie so much even you believe 'em
One can't fathom the shit that comes out your mouth
Yo, I'm calling you out
Lying comes easy to you
Thinking people actually believe you
Liar liar, please stop
You're no good at all
No need to say no more
Face it, do something 'bout it that's all!

Ask the Lord

As you look up giving praise
Ask the Lord to show you the way
Give you strength to go another day
Clarity and insight you're searching for
Hoping there's better
Needing peace in your soul
So you can keep pressing on
As you look up giving praise
Ask the Lord
Lord have your way
Weary in your works
Drained by your emotions
Waiting for the load to be lifted
Praying times be shifted
Asking for understanding seems small
You're tired of hitting a brick wall
As you look up giving praise
Ask the Lord to help you
Replenish your spirit today
Pressure felt in your bones
Destined to be alone
Tired of being tired for sure
This battle is not yours
Lift your hands up
Give it to the Lord!

Lonely Nights

Lonely nights come, they go
Lonely hearts bleed internally dying slow
This lonely heart in need to survive
Lonely heart why

Lonely nights come, they go
Joy comes in a new day
Leave last night behind
This loneliness is a phase

It is temporary
Give thanks for today
It's mandatory
He'll take away your loneliness
When you give him the Praise and Glory!

Farewell

As I looked toward the sky today
I thought of your journey knowing
The Lord is guiding you along the way
You're free from all the pain and worries
Of this world
You're safe and secure
Now in heaven with our Lord
Only if we could have you in our presence
For a moment or another day
We'll hold on to the memory
Of your laid back style
Never to forget your charm, your smile
Each and every day you will be missed so much
In our hearts you will remain
Life without you just won't be the same
We will cherish the caring generous man you have been
We'll see you next lifetime
Where we shall meet again
Farewell
Brother, father, grandfather, uncle,
Farewell Friend!

Nobody Knows

Was it easy to let go
You said you cared
Your feelings you've shown
Nobody knew it was you in her life
You remained a mystery
She continued giving her love to you
There was no strife
You said it's over
Then walked out her life
You were never for her
You forgot to mention you had a wife
This was just another scenario of how love can go
It served its purpose
That's why nobody knows!

Selfish Ways

Attempting to provoke her
She refuses to lose control
She'll kill you with her kindness
Remaining to keep her cool
She knows the odds of your intentions
You're always up to no good
Your selfish ways results in hurting
Someone over and over again
There's no valid motive
For your cycle of selfish ways
Be careful how you treat people
It'll catch up to you sooner or later
So don't cut off your nose
To spite your face
One day when you really need a friend
The bridges you burn
Will leave you in an empty place
Alone with nobody
Except you and your selfish ways!

Overdrive

What are these convictions filling your dome
Don't know how to deal
You're in overload
Your heart is beating fast
Damn, needing out to forget about the past
Trouble taking over your mind state
The pain is too great
Inside you've tried to deny
Withstanding life's roller coaster ride
What is your fate?
Emptiness in vast measures
These convictions has you in overload
Your heart racing in full speed
Unable to see what's ahead!

Beaten & Broken Down

Beaten and broken down
Physically, mentally, and emotionally
Too many women, men, and children losing sight
Living in a world where everything's a fight
Too many cases found
In a society filled with fear
These young girls mistreated
With a child to bare
Living off the system we call "welfare"
Overrated, understated
still beaten and broken down
Physically, mentally, and emotionally
In a world where our young brothers
Are dying younger everyday
The streets taking over
Gun battles, drugs, suicide cases
It doesn't have to be this way
Let's face this, our people's future
A sight frightening to see
Beaten and broken down
Physically, mentally, and emotionally!

Mr. Lonely

Hey there Mr. Lonely
So we meet again
Looking out the window
Watching the way of the wind
Finding it is you that seems
To be my only friend
Daydreaming of what would be nice
Longing for a little romance
One day in this lifetime
Yet it is you Mr. Lonely
That will not stray away
Mr. Lonely I don't want you hindering me
Go away
Let me be
Mr. Lonely you're not a part of me
Mr. Lonely
You're not a part of me

Never Far Away

Momma,
I'm not the one to question
Lord why
I know you'll be safe
In that beautiful kingdom in the sky
Looking forward to seeing you again
Missing you dearly
My Mother, my friend
I keep you in my thoughts
I pray believing
Having you in my heart
You'll never be far away!

Raped

Raped at 13 years old
Her pureness stolen
Hurting stripped of her innocents
Now pregnant having to deal with it
A heavy load and burden
Raped left baring a child on her own
Holding in her feelings
Like a lonely bird locked in a cage
Her laughter and smiles turned into rage
With no option or clue it was coming
Raped, made a victim
By a family member's cousin
Reminded every day
When she looks at her child
The baby has his face even his smile
Being stigmatized this way
To get through it she must continually pray
It wasn't her fault
That person was past being sick
It doesn't change the fact
A horrible incident raped
-Something she will never forget!

Endurance

Enduring the highs and lows
In-love with someone who one minute
Loves you so much
In the same breath won't embrace
Your loving touch what the fuck
You're feeling at times used and abused
However that same person
You don't want to lose
When it's good, great
When it's bad you hate to think
Could it be a mistake?
Maybe it's a dream
Open your eyes you're awake
An awesome individual you've been
She/he needs to return the love given
Tomorrow isn't promised cherish today
Stand firm decide if you will
Continue this way!

Hater Why

Are you a hater?
Look at the bigger picture
There's more to life & it's much greater
Than being your common hater
This doesn't apply to everyone
Hi haters don't act stunned
Hating on someone for what
If over a woman/man what the fuck
Dick come a dime a dozen
Coochie not that far from it
Why are you a hater?
Is it how they walk, talk, or look
What they got, who they are, and you're not
Is it that you don't know, can't remember you forgot
Look at the bigger picture
Giving a shout out to all the haters
For being so many other peoples motivators
It takes energy to be a hater
A miserable individual wasting their time
Redirect your thoughts
Life's too short
Don't dwell on petty things
The bigger picture is life has much greater things!

Name Calling

Why call women bitches & hoes
Is it the thing to say you suppose?
It matters what you call her
It matters what she answers to
Never should it be a bitch or a hoe
No matter how she's viewed
Our men should be treated like kings
Our women like queens
Time to start looking & talking
To women differently
Not labeled a bitch or hoe
Be it a family member, girlfriend, friend, or foe
Let the young girls and ladies know
You shouldn't talk like that to them
Don't settle
That's where it begins
Verbal abuse-name calling-must end
Reality is
We all come from a woman!

Her Lover, Her Friend

You're her lover, her friend
What's happening?
You're making this hard for her
Her love runs constant for you
Slowly you're trying to push her away
She's drifting
Help her comprehend the pain you're in
You're her lover, her friend
Will your love become a recollection?
On what you've built day to day
Do you want her to leave?
Do you want her to stay?
You're her lover, her friend,
This case she's pleading
To you
-does this have any meaning?

In the Mist of the Storm

In the mist of the storm
Trying to hold on,
As the clouds and dreary days
Don't seem to vanish
Still in the mist of the storm
You press on
Waiting for the day
The sun will shine
Leaving the mist of the storm behind
There are so many people suffering everyday
Without food nor shelter
Somebody help them you pray
Give them a way out
Provide opportunities so they can see all that they can be
Waiting to leave the mist of the storm
Seek relief from the pain and poverty
The clouds can be so dark
Hold on to faith, have hope in your heart
It won't happen overnight
The day is coming
Where you will see the rainbow in the sun shine brightly!

Shed Past Burdens

"In order to move FORWARD, we must learn to FORGIVE ourselves and others so that we do not stunt our own GROWTH."

-Unique

Inspirational

We all come across some trials and tribulations
Know with God in our lives, we will reach our destination
Times may look bad and things are all wrong
-hold on
He'll bring you peace, it won't be long
We tend to lose faith
We must believe in the Word
God is great, there's no one higher
He should be our biggest desire
Stop. Pray.
Without him in your heart and soul,
Things will never be in control.

Recognize

Lay it on the table
Let it go, let it die
Accept that you're through, don't wonder why
You thought she was a dime, your #1 boo
The truth is she wasn't woman enough for you
Let it go, let it die
You were living a lie
She didn't explain nor try
Left without saying good-bye
Took everything left you high & dry
This is chapter's end
Too bad you parted not as friends
Bump her, she's a crumbled leaf
Let her fly away with the wind!

Play the Hand

Girlfriend, get it the game
Play the hand you're dealt
Bump dude and what you felt
While in bed watching a flick
His phone rang late night
It's some other chick
Talking bout she's on her way over
He didn't put up much of a fight
Looked in your eyes
Told you, you gotta go then
Walked to the door and left it open
The nerve of him
Girlfriend, get in the game
Play the hand you are dealt
Get rid of him first
Then deal with what you felt
The amount of hurt there's no justification
Later for how he keeps your heart racing
Trust, somebody else can replace him
Later for you getting flushed when he speaks
Dump dat dude dats draining you
He's making you weak
Of course easier said than done
Run Caroline run
Run towards the light
Bounce back don't wait

If you're ever gonna get past it & heal
Bump what you once felt and still feel

Lifelong Lie

Mystified by the lie
Someone else created
Who are you? It's speculated
What could be the alibi for a lifelong lie?
Years of no sense of belonging
Tears shed due to not knowing
A father or mother you'd been longing
Time to take control
Done living out this lie
Healing begins here
It'll never change what you're about
The lie is out
You're aware
It doesn't matter anymore
Because although they were always near
This woman your mother, or this man your father
For you,
Had never been there!

Closure

Once what was, has come to its end
Forgetting what made us fall in- love
We tried it didn't work out
Acceptance.

Closure
You're no longer my husband/wife
Refusing being mistreated any longer
I walked out the door
Cuz baby I love myself more
Damn right
You're not a concern
It's been over were through
I had my closure the very day I left you!

Unspoken Words

Your heart has been broken
Never let what's bothering you go unspoken
Take heed to these words
As they roll out her my mouth
You don't have to be here
Get the hell out
You got caught in your game
It will never be the same
What nerve to think her love would remain?
Love, she's not a fool for you
Love don't live here
Handle that truth
Don't run back
When you realize the grass is not always greener
She's telling you she'll catch a charge
A felony or class A misdemeanor
It hurts like hell but she'll be fine
Don't ring her bell
Now the words haven't gone unspoken
She wishes you well!

A Time

There had been a time
When you hit rock bottom
In a selfless pit
With the faith you already possessed
It turned around
You're in the Lord's hands
He got it
You rid yourself of the pain & frustration
Of that one situation
When the people you love
Left you while at your lowest
It was then that it became obvious
Finally, you're letting go of it
You were always destined to make it
It's you that should've never been under estimated
No more energy for fakeness
Keeping the ones that'll support you thru it all
Beginning to end
People that are truly genuine!

Rotten Apple

You opened up letting him in
For what
You couldn't see he really didn't give a fuck
You gave him the time saying to yourself
Maybe he could be mine
Only when he had the time
N it blew up in your face
Now you wish you could go back
Rewind, erase
Don't look back on what's already done
Fuck'em
He's just not the one
Your feelings will eventually die
Go ahead, it's okay to cry
He's the apple that fell from the tree already rotten
Soon he'll be a memory forgotten
So sister-friend keep your head high
It's been overdo wave good-bye do you
Set him free cause it wasn't meant to be
Fuck dat rotten apple
That fell from the tree!

Think Not

Who she wants
Definitely, not who you got
Please, stop
Refusing to get caught up in the headache
You and your so called man are about
Your problem should be with him
A problem with her......think not
You may want to consider getting out
All you go thru obviously he's half ass gone
Don't blame her
If you're not his only one
The drama is between the two of you
She's just the one that will let you know the truth
Don't get it confused, write it down, take note
Cuz you coming at her is a joke
Who she wants
Please, definitely not who you got
Think not!

Trust

Don't know how to be a friend
Don't know who to trust, who's sincere
It's bad when you can't trust your own cousin
Friendship is when things are tough
They'll have your back regardless
An open ear at times that's what they lack
They don't even know it
Someone sharing laughter and tears
Someone who'll help you face your fears
Someone you can tell all
Not being judged when you do your own thing
Someone who won't stab you in the back
The first chance they get
Someone who will help guide you if you fall off track
A true friend, valuing the relationship
Never shunning you
Trusting in you with no hesistation!

You Don't Matter

The real you revealed
A very negative & nasty being
Constantly pointing out
What's bad about others through your eyes
And still you don't matter
You are of no value
You have no meaning
Walkin' round like your shit don't stink
Man, that's a theory you should rethink
If you feel like you're big
Attempting to belittle a person
Trying to bring them down
Listen, in the end you're nobody
Someone wants to keep around
How they appear to you doesn't matter
You have no power
That's a lost battle
Your words nothing but babble
So look in the mirror analyze yourself
Your opinion is irrelevant
You don't matter what the hell!

Do You Run

Do you run when you know it feels good?
Putting up your guard, making it complicated
Do you run when you know it feels good?
Have you ever felt for someone?
The thought takes you there
Remember the attraction
You go off mystery stare
Do you run?
Go with it, have some fun
It can be the simple pleasures, loving someone
Try it no need to run
If it feels right
Give in to the feeling!

Flame

Writing about a love torn apart
Those who've experienced it may take it to heart
You were the light on the darkest night
The candle slowly burning
The shadow slowly fades
Realizing, there's no joy without sorrow
There's no love without pain
Fearing commitment
No satisfaction in only being content
To people together, seemed like forever
What's the pleasure?
Neither knew how to say good-bye
So they remained
As the wax hardens a diminishing flame
Internally your heart is crying
Both wanted more, it showed
It's a damn shame it's so hard to let go
It's a damn shame; the candle lost its flame!

No Good

You no good mo fo
Was 'bout to dig you a new asshole
With these words-
The time and energy you're not worth
You already know
Spittin' this angry shit you can't get mad
After all you did you lying nitwit
Seeing me next lifetime
You can forget
Thought you stole a heart
She/he would be all aching, torn up
Ha ha you'll get what you deserve
Karma is a bitch
There's a plan for you already on reserve
You lying nitwit
Be gone
Kick bricks!

Goodbye

Kiss love goodbye
Pondering why-
How love vanishes, disappears
Something all who experienced love, dread-
Kissing love goodbye
So you said-
Never wanting to let go
Promising next time to take it slow
So you say-
"I'm sending you off love, with one final kissing blow
I'm sending you off love, with one final kissing blow!"

No Games

Why sit there listening to that man's bull?
He can't be thinking, "She's what some call a chicken-head, or a fool"
To believe his lines, his weak ass game
Somebody please tell that man he's lame
Ain't no free coochie rides over here
Get out her face
You better go somewhere
Cats these days always playing games
Coming at you with "You look good babe, something about you, you're
different"
(get it)
All along, they only wanna like the clit
Rub up on ya with their mmm
-inch of a dick
Cum correct, be direct
No games necessary
It's contrary-
To taste the love
Get more than a rub
If you come correct, be direct
Then, you will get respect!

Holds No Weight

Love & sincerity
At times, holds no weight
Too often the good person finishes last
To get what you want, sometimes you have to show your ass
It doesn't pay being pleasant and nice
-people take you for granted
Your kindness taken as weakness
-speechless
You can treat someone good as gold
Nothing would you withhold
People are really too bold

Love & sincerity
At times, holds no weight
Some don't care what they do,
How they do it, or who they do it to
Causing chaos, they don't care
Actions prove it
-they're out for self
Not caring about anyone else
Love & sincerity
God will have your back, stand on faith
And in time, He will give you clarity & strength!

Mind-Surfin'

Sitting by the water
Taking in the view
Such a tranquil place to release
Your theories tumbling free, mind-surfin'
Thinking of dude
You still feel him
A hole in your heart
Filled with covet
Clearly it was nothing anyway
Blinded no more
Stop mind-surfin'
He's forever a memory!

Stop Playin'

Stop playing games
Say what you want upfront
It can be over before we start
I'm gonna say this once, I'm gonna be real blunt
Stop playing games
If it's me you want
Your nonsense, I'm not wit'
I can't please everybody all the time
If you don't perceive what I am saying
Oh well-
The problem is not mine
Not giving all to have my back against the wall
I don't wanna play
I quit-
No need to go through this
Player, player
Your game is pure bullshit!

Secluded Heart

A secluded heart, needing to be refreshed
-by a kind being
Someone compassionate and loyal
Have you in an uproar
Keeps the passion boiling, steaming
A secluded heart
Needing to be refreshed
Tired of emptiness
What must one do to find a love that's faithful
You understand oh too well
This secluded heart is yours
Only you didn't want to tell!

Ending the Ride

The ride is over
Revealing you're not a Casanova
Was wrong in her choice
Was wrong in her view
She must start anew
She'd given her best to you
A four leaf clover
You should've never parted with
This too will pass as before
Accepting what it was hitting for
You won't ever walk through her door
She should've seen it then
Farewell lover, farewell friend
The ride is over!

Enhance Self-Love

"LOVE starts with SELF & comes in various ways. We all need it; UNLEASH it."

-Unique

Magnificent Woman

A woman is magnificent in a sense
She provides a home for her kids
She has her own shit
Paying the bills where she lives
A woman with confidence
Reaching for the sky
There's no limit to a magnificent woman
Are you listening?
She has an inner gem
Not hidden or forbidden
Qualities of a true cutie
Doesn't need a man to define her
However, would like to have a man willing to walk beside her
Huh, she knows when to let a man be a man
Still holding it down ride or die
Not enough words for her to be described
She's magnificent
The one you'd want to keep beside you
So all the magnificent women out there
Snap your fingers to this
Although we're different shapes, colors, and sizes
Let these men know
A magnificent woman is here for sure!

What is Love?

What is love?
Feelings appeasing
Lost for words
Love.
Is it pain, peace, misery?
Is it delight within you or me?
That thing we call love
-Is it meant to be?
Sentiments of what you undergo
Detoured at times for love
Why is this?
Once again you see,
Longing for that thing we call love
Love and its complexity
Boggling
Searching what it is
You're being challenged!

Grounded

Many times you've waited
For someone to make you whole
Eventually, it will take its toll
Now you decide
Looking for love in self
No reward more satisfying
No emptiness, no crying, no guilt
Peace and ambition
Will make you complete
With faith, go ahead
Claim it for keeps
Don't ever wait on someone to please you
Turn your life around
Step out onto solid ground!

Grateful for Existence

A peaceful co-existence
Of this serenity which lies deep
Verbalizing her inner notion
"God blesses me"
She gives thanks to him
With no regrets
She lives day by day
Nobody said this would be easy
I know he didn't carry me this far to leave me!

Own Your Sexy

Acknowledge your sexy
-own it
Head held high
Sexy,
Confident
Feel it as you walk by
Indulge in your sexy
Body, soul, and mind
Glowing in your stance
Day in, day out, all the time
Sexy,
In the way you talk
Sexy is in your smile
That good feeling you know
-is critical
Amazing, breathtaking, worthwhile
Got to have your sexy daily
Don't give a damn
If heard from many or none,
Your sexy requires no approval
From anyone!

Free

Blue beauty, blue seas
Snow, rain, or sleet
Spirit be free
Oceans run deep
Mountains high
Unknown measures
Creativity occupies the mind?
Blue beauty, blue seas
Rainbows, clouds sun, and stars
Spirit be free
Appearing far
Unlimited capabilities of the heart
No boundaries
Blue beauty, blue seas
Spirit be free!

God Gives

Absorbing life each day
No matter the obstacles
Getting in the way
A smile suspends on this face
Energy like a plague
God gives
His words I'll take
Demeanor not of an impostor
Reminds us all things are possible
Inner beauty the scope
Scrutinizing my mirth
God determines our joy
God gives me and my kids hope
To Him I'll applaud!

The Zone

The stillness in the room
Before entering a zone- Don't bother me.

Needing to regroup
Not looking in life's rear view mirror
The stillness in the room is mines

This shouldn't take long maybe a minute of your time
Breathe, stretch, shake, proceed on
Breathe, stretch, shake
Nobody can take me out my zone

Setting the tone, calmness in my space
This down-time overdue
Relaxed where I want to be, me time
Without any explanation
Always take time

Take in the stillness
That's in the room then
Breathe, stretch, shake, enjoy your zone!

Revive

Invite and circulate yourself in positive energy
Walk out of the season of negativity
Observe, rationalize
People will leap in and out of your life
Transform into the person you want to be
Its relevance unveiled
Don't allow it to affect what makes you happy
Resuscitate your mental
Subsist abundantly
Glide into what shall be
Your sculpted destiny!

Me and My Thoughts

Where do I begin?
Where do I start?
I'm pulling from my gut
Giving insight to my thoughts
Bear with me
Sometimes I get choked up
Very passionate in all I do
This is a poem real to me
Yes, it's true
Stepping out the box of my normal routine
A need for more
Experiencing bigger things
There's a place out here for me
To live out my dreams
Writing and singing the few things I do
That's only naming my favorite two
If you want to know more
Set up a private interview

Awakened

Her spirit is alive
Awakened
-it doesn't bother her what you think
She can't be shaken
Everything about her is real
She's in love with herself
Head to toe, each and every curve
Her body she'll own
Not being vain
Her spirit is alive
Awakened
-She's not the smallest or the largest
Maybe not the best dressed
However,
She works with what she got
She always comes correct
Doing her own thing
Her spirit is alive, Awakened
That feeling is the best!

Worthy to be Loved

When a person genuinely loves you
They will not inflict intentional pain
It doesn't take away your smile
Smack or punch you in the face
Your "No" love doesn't violate
When a person genuinely respects you
They will not beat you down,
Bruise you, leave you black and blue
Love is kind, love is true
When someone genuinely **treasures you,**
They will ardor you for being you
It's a construction based on the many defining words:
Respect, Ardor, Cherish, Attachment, Infatuation, Treasure,
Admiration, Prize, Regard, Adore, and Rapture
Not painful physically, love doesn't hurt
Love should be lavishing
Love yourself enough
Realize what you're worth
Worthy to be loved.

UNIQUE

Sensationally UNIQUE where I stand
Here I am
Dreaming the best of dreams
No longer willing to put it on hold
Working on the one and only me
Stepping forward never again settling
Thriving to pass my expected goals
Watch how my final poem will be told
Huh, that's the best getting it done regardless

Sensationally UNIQUE where I stand here I am
Patiently I'll wait for one
Who'll feed my soul
Constantly
Unconditionally
I'm not high maintenance
I'm high quality
Continuing being the same either way
Always sensationally UNIQUE
Yesterday, tomorrow, today!

Growth in Process

Finally at the point in life
Where you have pacification
You thought you'd never find
Be thankful seeing your growth
You may not be where you want to be
You are no longer how or where you use to be
Whatever you go through
Whatever tests you must take
God does everything for a reason
It's not a mistake!

Hold Your Dream

Shooting star speed by
Advance into your retreat
Come glide with me
Grab on to who you want to be
Your dreams appear at a expanse
Yet at arm's length
Catch it with full depth

Shine brightly
Don't ever give up on your dreams
That one day can be
Look up
Watch the shooting star fly by
Continue to dream
Focus on all the prospects
Allow yourself to go after your dream!

We Are

Clasping inner jubilation
She's in the gist of the moon, sun and stars
A defining moment of who we are
Positioned
-her hand on the mic
Her words almost lyrical
Pay attention to-
The parable she'll recite
Profound experiences of hers and others
Various scenarios of life & love's struggles
Daughters, Sisters, Aunts, Mothers
What defines who we are
Neither past pain, hurt, bad times, nor concerns
Hope that someone will get insight from this book
Learn
Everything is not for our understanding
What will define us?
Not a person, place, or material things
-it's something grander
Lady knowledge informs us
We are strong, strong as we grow
Strong, independent women
Defining who we are
Gift wrapped, with a bow!

New Year, New Beginning

New year, New beginning
There's no stopping my growth
No rewind, fast forward, no ending
Won't hold back on the gift given
Look for a light to shine
That light, it'll be mine
No room for negativity or doubts
My growth consists of God, my kids, my Mom,
Sister, niece, nephew, my Auntie P
Prayer with TRUE friends TRUE family
Who've consistently been there for me
Shout out to them
The talent they'd always seen
What God has planned for me
Can't nobody stop
I'm happy within loving myself
Knowing my worth, who I am
Finally, knowing what it is about
This joy I'll take in
No rewind, fast forward, no ending
It's a new year a new beginning!

Love, You Are Who You Are

To luxuriate in a field
Where the trees look unreal
And the grass stands at a perfect dimension
Love,
You are who you are

Something stronger than
Other peoples' opinions
Standing firm in where you're conditioned

To luxuriate in a field
Where the trees look unreal
And the grass stands at a perfect dimension
Love,
You are who you are

Something realer than the word L.O.V.E.
In constant growth daily
Love,
You are who you are
No if's ands or maybes!

Waste No More of My Pretty

Waste no more of my pretty
I have feelings like you
You can't treat me like a dishcloth, you betta decide
-if it's me you really want fool
I'm a person very rare
You can try, few have been compared
I've tried being tolerant of you and what you've demanded
My heart hurting blow by blow
It's bleeding in doing so
Can't stand it
Waste no more of my pretty
What the hell is the madness
Loving you absolutely was easy, with such gladness
It's got to be about me today
Time to do it my way
No more wasting my pre-ttay!

Your Love

Your love keeps my heart
Without it-
Would feelings continue to sprout?
Turning the unknown into perspective
Without it-
I'd have no sight unrealistic objectives
Your love wakes me daily
Takes away any distress that comes my way
Makes me want to continue to write and sing
Without it-
Never would you've heard a thing
Your love found me
Made me desire more
Believe me,
Your love I do adore
I give thanks to you Lord!

I'm a Friend

Loving hard when you love
Never jealous, never selfish
Faithful and proud
Valuing every relationship
Not vain, not boasting
Respectful, empathetic, inspiring
No matter the cost
Giving 150 percent
Always helpful, always sincere
Descriptions of myself
A true and precious friend!

Savor Being Erogenous

"Being comfortable with your own sexuality enables you to find pleasure in the experience"

Daydreaming

Watching from across the room
Will he notice soon
She wants to go off to a place
Wishing it won't be hard to find

Craving him, picturing their bodies fused
Giving him access
Daydreaming he's the one to give good loving
Juices surging

Damn this is some shit
She hasn't met him
Daydreaming
Of this guy she wants get with and can't forget!

Foreplay

With no entry
His touch brings a single tear
You get a rush
There's that tingle
Gently, he clutches your face
Your lips bound together at a slow gait
He strokes your head with such detail
Kissing your neck
Fondling your breast
There's that throbbing
-your wet
Wanting him at that instant
Resistance is hard
He starts whispering the nasty shit
"Oh Claud"
Asking you if you can handle it, mmmmm…
There's that chill
Resistance was your test
All ready for the rest
He wasn't done
Spreading your legs, lightly kissing your inner-thigh
There's the unexplainable high
Wait oooh you sigh
Mmm he's lightly blowing on your skin
You want him to come in
He flips you over massaging your back

"aahh"
There's that throbbing, tingling chill again
No more foreplay
You gotta have him!

The Ride

Mmm, mmm, mmm, my my my
I get on this rollercoaster ride
It's called the magic-stick
I enjoy it because it's never over too quick
You know when you're climbing the highest hill
And you reach the top, then you drop
-that's the feeling I get from the beginning
An astonishing rush
What a feeling inside
Mmm, mmm, mmm, my my my
I can't seem to get enough of this ride
I'd be so free
I'd let the ride take over me
Getting on without holding on, such a natural high
One of the greatest rollercoaster rides

Each time I ride it, it's never the same
Hold up-
I just came
-back around to go up again
So when I get off and it gets shut down
I look forward to getting back on it when next weekend comes around
If only it was mine
I would ride it everyday
Every chance I get, I take
'cause the magic-stick
Mmm, mmm, mmm, my my my, is the shit!

Are You Cumin'?

I'll cum if you cum
Where-ever-we-are
Willing and capable
If in your office, car, or store
If on an open floor
If in your yard in the dark
After hours in the park
On a swing, slide, or rock
I'll cum if you cum
Are you cumin
Anywhere, anytime
If on your porch if in your house
We can cum together
Let it squirt out
Turn over, enjoy the sexual high
That's that good shit, right, right!

Naughty

Resting on my bed
Enjoying the breeze from the fan
I got this sensation
Naughty thoughts
-oh man
In need of a workout
You know upfront
It ain't good if you can't make me shout
Dim the lights, do your thing
Take it from the bed to the floor
In your ear I'll softly sing "More"
Whisper my name quietly
I'll let you taste mi amore
Meet me in the bubble bath
Where the candles are lit, the fruit and champagne is chillin
What better than to clean it, lick it, eat it, wasn't that fulfilling!

Pleasurable Pain

I enjoy the sound of the rain
I enjoy a little pleasurable pain
I want your good loving
You're soothing
Your swagger is wild
-won't hover over you
However, I'm diggin' your technique
If you were here
We'd be straight fuckin'
To the twine fiercely blowing
The rain against the window pane
The sound of the storm turning me on
Can't be tamed, won't be tamed
Damn, I'm pining some of that pleasurable pain
It's making me dampened
Come over, together let's break a sweat
Can you stand the rain, or are you not ready yet?
A lovely sound, grinding to the rain cumin' down
The thought
"oooh aaah"
Wait-
My _____throbbing
There she goes, no stopping
I came!
So come over, let's enjoy the sound of the rain
Give me the realness
Of your pleasurable pain!

96

Mental Orgasm

She was listening
Stunned at dude's swagger
What he called a "mental orgasm"
You can't imagine
Don't talk about it be about it
Mental orgasm
With just a glance of you, she'd be ready to take off her pants
-it's true
Have her dripping right now
-can't hold back
That's a real mental orgasm
-when you haven't even touched her yet
Already you got her flowing, drenched before the head of your cock touches
her warm walls
She's near her climax
You may pass the test
When you dig deeper into your sexual intellect
Mental orgasm
Look into the definition
Let's not mention how he came off
With what he can do
Understand he may be good
However, she's tryna school you
Yeah, he might lick the na na right
Think he's bangin' her in a blazing position
Aight

Is it a physical or mental orgasm? Which one?
'cause she can cum multiple times, hop right back on the dick
Have that one tear fall down your face
Your toes curl up & shit
In your mind you still be wanting it
But your dick ain't ready for that good shit
No need to call Tyrone
You better call Viagra or Cialis quick!
Pump, pump, pump, pump it up
Women know how to fake it
Was it really a mental orgasm?

Mesmerized

Drowning in the emotions
Gazing into your core
Mesmerized by the way
You invigorate her
The word "No" doesn't apply
When it comes to you
A perception she'll attempt to portray
What goes through her body
As she gazes into your core
Mesmerized every time more and more

Whether looking at you from a distance
Or a brief glance of your face
You're electrifying
Your flavor she loves to taste
Trying to stay atop
Drowning in the emotions felt
Gazing into your core
Mesmerized by you
Every time always more and more!

In His Realm

Sunshine Sunshine
Its morning
He lays there beside you
You're in his realm
He's capturing the inner qualities of you
Tell him what you want from him
Enjoy his temperament, sit by a fire
Sipping
Taking each other higher
Make love til' the break of day
Stop, he'll never hear you say
Let him caress you with his tender touch
Show you the way to the pleasures he'll bring
No Rush!!!!
He goes in with deep penetration
He'll have you speaking different languages
Saying
Tae ki era mucho mi amore'
His tasty-yet-succulent-spice
Trickling, embracing you til' you drop
You're in his realm!

About You

About you
Little things you do
You're strong, gentle, breath taking
I've waited for so long
Can't hold back the temptation
I'm at the highest elevation
With you
I'm on the highest tower
Like a butterfly flying unconstrained
Making love to me mentally
About you
I feel like spreading my wings
Every time, every time I see you
It's a different kind of thing
Baby, you give me an urge
About you
You and what you bring
Finding myself thinking of you
I enjoy the phrase: "Quality Time"
Under the stillness of the moonlit skies
The gleam upon your face
Only you only you
Have taken me to the most sensuous place
It is you
About you!

One Hell of a Guy

Late night.
Strange, you're on her mind
So familiar you are with her
You've set the bar
No other has come close to
She's missing you
Oh my, you're one hell of a guy
The vibe is explosive
The hugs, when you run your fingers slowly down her spine
How do you, each time
It's so fresh, so new
You know what to say, just what to do
-and the right spots
You lift her spirits, make her shiver
It never took much
Can't get enough, can't hold it inside
You're one hell of a guy!

Thirst

Sleek in how he pulled her in
With ease
Delighted in disrobing her
Inch by inch
Her body he was exploring
Her thirst he wants to quench
Gripping her breast
Mouth, tongue, and her fingers connect
Gradually entering her juicy walls
Deeper and deeper
He crawled
Her sap flows like a waterfall
Both drenched
Her thirst he delectably had quenched!

Your Arms Around Me

Loving your arms wrapped around me
Giving into you completely
What we share isn't a surprise
Partaking in our time
As it is meant to be
Concentrating on the rapture of you and me
Loving your arms around me-
Loving your arms wrapped around me!

The Distance

Ooh la la mi amore
My imagination is running away with me
Although there's distance between us
I'm feeling you, as if you were near
Your voice I'm awaiting to hear
Yet the distance keeps me wanting you,
Yearning for you
The distance won't stop us
Thinking how you embrace me
The way you'd caress me nice and slowly
Ooh la la mi amore
Missing how you make me smile
It's been a while
You know the things we do
When it's just me and you
For the love you give me
For the love I give to you
Ooh la la mi amore
Be it your will
Although there's distance between us
At that very moment
You were here for real!

Quickie

All night I've hungered to kiss your lips
Come closer, lay back flow with it
Listen, that's the jam playing
Let me do as I please
Relax a minute, be easy
Your pith not to be matched
Simply, I'm attached
My attention on you, your attention on me
Be quiet,
The party's still going on downstairs
Don't want to sound the alarm
Don't make a peep
Quickly, undress me, bend me over
Gripping me,
Thrusting at a perfect pace
Clear the desk change place
Exalting the sensation
Now it's time we get back to the celebration!

About the Author

I was born into the world prematurely on April 10, 1973 as Tiffany April Cooper in NY, NY. At that very moment it was evident that the Lord had plans for me. I was raised in New Rochelle, N.Y. Growing up, there weren't too many things I didn't want to do. I've been blessed with many talents which were noticed early on. At the age of 6 I began singing, at age 7 I began cheerleading for Pop Warner Football League for about 7 years. I held the position of captain once I got older. It was then that I learned from my cheerleading "Moms" never to use the word CAN'T; it means that you WON'T, and that was not acceptable. They also taught me that when you do something you must practice and push yourself even at times when you don't feel like it. The end results will always show the hard work and dedication you put into it. I have had many wonderful experiences. I am grateful for each and every one.

I practiced tap, ballet, flute, and piano. I attended the affiliated school of Julliard School of Music in New York City. I began writing at thirteen. It was at that time I was fortunate to be offered to sing professionally. I chose not to because I was not ready for the pressures that would come along with it. Then thereafter I was recommended by my school's principal to run for Miss New York's Perfect Teen. I had to write an auto-biography about myself to get accepted. Never did I imagine I would be chosen. There was a weekend retreat about the starvation in the world where only two students were picked to go from each city; I was selected.

I have never been one to take things for granted. Although I have done so much I have also had some bumps in the road along the way just like anybody else. Writing has always been a passion and escape for me. I decided to write this book to share the different thoughts and feelings of mine and others in the simplest way. Not everyone can express themselves. Feelings are what they are and should not be ignored. I'm not ashamed nor shy to share where I've been and where I'm going. I hope that whoever reads this book of poetry will smile and say "WOW"!

"I'm not writing for the money, finally,
I'm writing for the love of me!"

-Unique